Introduction

In January 2012, the United States announced a strategic shift towards the Asia-Pacific because U.S. economic and security interests are increasingly linked to developments in Asia.[1] In the twenty years since the collapse of Soviet Communism, U.S. strategy in Asia increasingly focused on the rise of the People's Republic of China (PRC). However, the US failed to include another major country in Asia, Russia. America placed Russia and China into two separate strategies for Europe and Asia respectively. The US intended to separate China and Russia but instead, Beijing and Moscow have substantially improved relations over the past twenty years and entered a new strategic partnership. Analysts now predict that China and Russia will form a future strategic alliance and the United States will fight a future war against a Chinese-Russian bloc.[2] Sino-Russian relations, past and present, are an important feature of major power relations in Asia. China and Russia have maintained tense relations throughout their history, but seized opportunities to form strategic partnerships when their interests aligned. During the Cold War, Moscow and Beijing formed a Sino-Soviet alliance that significantly complicated U.S. strategy in Asia. The United States learned to manage the US-China-Russia triangular relationship as part of U.S. Cold War strategy. After the Sino-Soviet split, the US made a major foreign policy reversal improving relations with China as a strategic counterweight against the Soviet Union. While China and Russia develop their new "strategic partnership," American foreign policymakers ought to rediscover the importance of Sino-Russian relations. As the United States pivots toward Asia, U.S. national security professionals must include Russia and Sino-Russian relations as a vital part of any strategy to manage China.

Russia's Place in Asia, Next to China

Russia is a European country, but it is also a part of Asia. Approximately two thirds of the Russian Federation is located in Asia to include a 2,700 mile border with China, the longest land border in the world.[3] Spanning the Eurasian land mass, Russia is Europe's link to the

Pacific Ocean. Beyond geography, approximately 21 percent of Russians culturally identify

themselves as Asian vice European.[4] Russia is not merely a part of Asia.

Russia is a traditional Asian power, and throughout its modern history, Russia actively

participated in the geo-politics of the region. Beginning in the nineteenth century, Russia

expanded into the Far East resulting in territorial disputes with other Asian powers. Japan, one

of these powers, still disputes ownership of the Southern Kuril Islands with Russia. In the

twentieth century, Russia fought or supported wars involving China, Japan, India, the Koreas,

and Vietnam. Russia has long perceived important and at times vital national interests in Asia.

Today, Russian leaders are expanding economic ties with Asia. In July 2010, the Russian

government adopted a $60 billion plan to develop Siberia in the Russian Far East. This

development strategy, which extends out to the year 2020, develops infrastructure so Russia can

realize its economic potential in the Asia-Pacific region.[5] Dmitri Trenin, Director of the

Carnegie Moscow Center, advocates a more significant shift to the east recommending that

Russia consider Vladivostok its "twenty-first-century capital."[6]

Moscow also wants to be perceived as a leader in the region. Russia participates in Asian

multilateral forums to include the Association of Southeast Asian Nations (ASEAN) Regional

Forum, the Six Party Talks, the East Asia Summit, and the Shanghai Cooperative Organization

(SCO). In 2012, Russia will host the Asia-Pacific Economic Cooperation (APEC) conference on

Russky Island off of the coast of Vladivostok.

Russia shared relations with several Asian powers throughout its modern history, but no

relationship was more significant than Russia's connection to China. The interaction of China

and Russia is a central theme in the history of great power relations in Asia. The United States

realized this during the Cold War when the Soviet Union and PRC formed the Sino-Soviet alliance. In the future, Sino-Russian relations will be no less important. Russia's place in Asia is alongside China.

Sino-Russian Relations

Rosemary Quested concluded her work on Russian expansion in East Asia with the following commentary on Sino-Russian relations, "Though deeply alien to one another in race, culture, history, and with many . . . sources of discord between them, Russia and China are compelled to live as neighbors in a jostling globe to face an inscrutable future."[7] Throughout their history, China and Russia maintained tense relations but forged alliances in response to common threats. In addition, the two countries shaped relations with each other in response to the larger geo-political situation in Asia. Therefore, one cannot completely understand Chinese or Russian foreign policy without surveying the interaction of the two.

In the middle of the nineteenth century, Russia began a process of eastward expansion that established the context of Sino-Russian relations for the next 150 years. Between 1858 and 1860, Russia joined Britain and France in imposing a series of "unequal treaties" on China.[8] In addition to trade concessions, Russia also took over a million square kilometers of territory including portions of China's western border near Xinjiang and the Maritime Province to the east that included the modern day city of Vladivostok. Later in 1898, Russia seized the southern tip of the Liaodong Peninsula securing the ice free port at Lushun (Port Arthur).

Russia continued this expansion during the twentieth century. In the final days of the Second World War, 1.5 million Soviet troops occupied Manchuria and North Korea. On August 14, 1945, the same day that Japan surrendered, Joseph Stalin signed a treaty with Chiang Kai-shek giving Russia control of key railroads and ports in Manchuria.[9] Stalin also occupied Outer Mongolia with 100,000 men as Soviet advisors took over the government in Ulan Bator. Engineered by the Soviets, Outer Mongolia held a referendum on October 25, 1945 in which

98.4 percent of eligible voters favored independence from China. The Nationalist government formally recognized the independence of Outer Mongolia in January of the following year.[10]

In 1950, as Mao Zedong and Joseph Stalin initiated a Sino-Soviet alliance, Stalin forced territorial concessions on Mao under the terms of the Sino-Soviet Treaty of Friendship, Alliance and Mutual Assistance. Later in 1969, the Soviet Union and China came to the brink of major war along the border contributing to the Sino-Soviet split. After the Cold War, China and Russia settled their border dispute in July 2008. However, Russia still occupies a vast amount of Chinese territory, and the potential for conflict still remains.

China and Russia developed their relationship in an environment of tension and mistrust, but when necessary, the two formed strategic alliances in response to common threats. As Japan expanded onto the Asian mainland, China and Russia joined forces to counter Japanese expansion. In 1896, the two nations entered a short lived alliance after Japan defeated China in the Sino-Japanese War of 1894-1895. Later in 1931, the Soviet Union and Nationalist China signed a non-aggression pact as Japanese forces invaded Manchuria. During the Japanese occupation of China, the Soviet Union provided military assistance to both the Guomindang (GMD) and Chinese Communist Party (CCP) who had joined forces forming the Second United Front.

After World War II, the United States replaced Japan as the binding element of a Sino-Soviet partnership. The Chinese Civil War resumed in 1947 as GMD and CCP forces dissolved the Second United Front. The United States backed the Nationalists, and the Soviet Union supported the CCP. Following the communist victory in 1949, Mao Zedong leaned towards the Soviet Union based on common interests and ideology. Thereafter, the US faced the combined weight of the Sino-Soviet alliance in Asia for twenty years. In those two decades, the PRC and

Soviet Union supported North Korea and North Vietnam in two major wars against the United States.

China and Russia calculated their alliance based on national interests, but also adjusted their relationship in response to broader geopolitics. At the turn of the twentieth century, Russia joined China opposing Japanese expansion into East Asia. However, Russia later allied with Japan in 1914 allowing Russian military forces to shift from Asia to Europe during the First World War. During World War II, the Soviet Union signed a neutrality pact with Japan in 1941 for the same motive. China also responded to changing geopolitics. In the middle of the Cold War, Beijing dissolved its alliance with the Soviet Union after the United States redefined US-China relations.

Throughout this history, China and Russia set aside differences and established alliances when necessary. Another conclusion is apparent. Geo-political factors heavily influenced the relationship between China and Russia. After the Soviet Union collapsed, the United States was the nation most capable of shaping future Sino-Russian relations. However, U.S. strategy poorly managed the relationship between Russia and China, and the two Asian powers entered a new phase of strategic partnership.

Post-Cold War U.S. Strategy: China in the East, Russia in the West

In the Post-Cold War era, U.S. foreign policy largely ignored Russia's role in Asia. America placed Russia and China into two separate foreign policy problem sets. After the collapse of the Soviet Union, the United States made Russia the center of a strategy for Europe. Meanwhile, U.S. policy for Asia acted to balance a rising China. However, the US lacked an overarching grand strategy to synchronize the two independent strategic aims. U.S. strategy, or the lack thereof, effectively isolated Russia in Europe and contained China in Asia. As a result, the United States contributed to the current phase of Sino-Russian rapprochement.[11]

President William J. Clinton established the post-Cold War U.S. approach to Asia. As policymakers debated the role of the US after the Cold War, Clinton unveiled a policy for enlarging U.S. engagement in the East Asia and Pacific region. America set three objectives for Asia. First, the US remained committed to its treaty allies in the Pacific: Australia, Japan, the Philippines, South Korea, and Thailand. Second, America maintained its troop presence in the region. Finally, the US fostered development and participation in multilateral institutions.[12] Generally, the United States continues to adhere to the strategic approach laid out by Clinton.

Over time, Beijing expanded its power and U.S. policy increasingly focused on China in Asia. China engineered decades of economic growth enabling it to compete with the United States. Beijing also directed Chinese military expansion and modernization prompting U.S. officials to claim that China lacked transparency and contributed to regional insecurity. America also questioned the intent of China's military modernization as Beijing deployed the People's Liberation Army Navy in support of Chinese territorial demands in the South China Sea. China extended a claim to the to the "second island chain" creating overlapping rights to the Spratley and Paracel Islands with several Asian governments.[13] The rise of China compelled U.S. policymakers to increasingly make Beijing the focus of strategy formulation for Asia.

U.S. policymakers adopted an ad-hoc approach to China pursuing policies that fell between engagement and containment.[14] Official U.S. policy supported the peaceful rise of a "responsible" China into the international community.[15] However, Beijing feared that the US sought to contain China.[16] In addition to the pre-existing U.S. alliance structure in Asia, America also improved bi-lateral relations with India and Vietnam, two of China's traditional rivals. President Obama only increased Chinese concerns in 2012 by issuing defense guidance to shift focus to the Asia-Pacific. China sensed encirclement by the US from many directions, but not from Russia.

Over the past twenty years, the United States gradually ignored Russia in the formulation of Asia-Pacific policy. In 1998, America recognized Russia in U.S. defense policy for Asia stating, "As an Asia-Pacific power with a substantial presence and relevance to the security of the region, Russia's open and constructive participation in regional security affairs will remain in the U.S. national interest."[17] In contrast, the latest strategic guidance for the U.S. Department of Defense in 2012 makes no mention of Russia in the pivot towards the Asia-Pacific region. The document mentions Russia only once, but in the context of U.S. commitments in Europe.[18] In November 2011, U.S. Secretary of State Hillary Clinton published an article entitled *America's Pacific Century*, outlining the new U.S. focus on Asia. The word "Russia" did not appear in the article.[19]

U.S. policymakers did focus on Russia, but in Europe not Asia. After the collapse of the Soviet Union, both Moscow and the US sought to incorporate Russia into the west through political and economic reforms. President Clinton planned to gradually include Russia into a newly expanded North Atlantic Treaty Organization (NATO) through Russian participation in consultative bodies such as the Partnership for Peace.[20] The US provided economic assistance to the Russian Federation, but did little else to integrate Russia into Europe. Instead of incorporating Russia, NATO expanded eastward into Russia. Thus, NATO followed a policy of containment against the Soviet Union during the Cold War and continued this policy even after the Cold War ended.[21]

According to Dmitri Trenin, U.S. policy towards Russia caused Moscow to abandon its goal of joining the west.[22] Prime Minister Vladimir Putin came to power in 2000 and shifted to a new strategy of asserting influence closer to home, particularly in the Commonwealth of Independent States (CIS).[23] Putin pursued an independent foreign policy increasingly placing Russia at odds with America. As a result, US-Russia relations deteriorated. In 2003, Russia joined the "coalition of the unwilling" opposing the U.S. invasion of Iraq. Later, Russia protested the U.S. military presence in Central Asia and opposed U.S. sanctions on Iran. In 2008, Russia launched a military intervention against the Republic of Georgia in South Ossetia marking a low point in US-Russia relations.

America pursued separate strategies for Europe and Asia disregarding Russia's links to China and the rest of the Asia-Pacific. U.S. policymakers balanced against China in Asia and isolated Russia in Europe. With the exception of supporting Russian participation in Asia-Pacific multilateral forums, the US established few policies to shape Russia's role in Asia.[24]

Two outcomes resulted from the U.S. strategic approach to Europe and Asia after the Cold War. First, U.S. policymakers failed to recognize Russia's role in the Asia-Pacific and the U.S. military followed suit. Given its place as a bridge between Europe and Asia, it is difficult to assign Russia to a single geographic region. The U.S. military's Unified Campaign Plan (UCP) attempted to do just that, placing all of Russia within the United States European Command (USEUCOM).[25] In 2009, the United States Pacific Command (USPACOM) organized five Strategic Focus Groups (SFGs) reflecting the command's priorities. Russia, with its relatively capable Pacific armed forces, did not make the list.[26]

Second, the United States unwittingly encouraged China and Russia to forge closer ties. Since the end of the Cold War, China and Russia formed the closest relationship between the two in the history of Sino-Russian relations.[27] America isolated Russia in Europe, so Moscow increasingly looked towards the Far East.[28] In the past, Russia and China did not form alliances naturally, but rather when faced by common adversaries. In the Cold War, China and the Soviet Union formed an alliance against a shared U.S. threat. Twenty years after the end of the Cold War, China and Russia, once again, are forming a Sino-Russian bloc to counter the United States.

A New Sino-Russian Strategic Partnership

Despite America's preference to treat China and Russia separately, the two countries have formed a significant partnership since the end of the Cold War. Through a series of summits, Russia and China established friendly relations throughout the 1990s. In 2001, the two nations formalized their "strategic partnership" signing the Treaty of Good-Neighborliness and Friendly Cooperation. The treaty included provisions for no first use of nuclear weapons, military cooperation, and respect for "national unity and territorial integrity."[29] In 2008, Russia and China negotiated an agreement on the formerly disputed islands of Yinlong (Tabarov) and Heixiazi (Bolshoi Ussurisky) in the Amur River, the last of many steps to finally resolve a four decade long border dispute.[30] Both Russia and China point out that this "strategic partnership" is not a "strategic alliance." Regardless, China and Russia have significantly improved diplomatic, economic, and military relations in the post-Cold War era.

Diplomatically, China and Russia increasingly share similar positions in international affairs, especially their commitment to counter U.S hegemony.[31] In May 2008, the two countries released the *Joint Statement of the People's Republic of China and the Russian Federation on Major International Issues*.[32] Clearly directed at the US, Beijing and Moscow called for a multipolar world and denounced "frequent regional conflicts" caused by "unilateralism."[33] China and Russia also use their permanent seats on the United Nations Security Council to shape this agenda. China expert Minxin Pei claims that Moscow and Beijing have created a "Russia-China axis of obstruction" in the Security Council.[34] Most recently in February 2012, both China and Russia vetoed an Arab and Western backed resolution condemning the government of President Bashar al Assad of Syria. China has little interest in Syria, but gave priority to supporting Russian interests in Syria over maintaining positive relations with the US.

China and Russia also extended joint diplomacy to counter US and NATO interests in Central Asia. Beijing and Moscow formed the Shanghai Cooperation Organization (SCO) in June 2001 consisting of six member nations: China, Russia, Kazakhstan, Kyrgyzstan, Tajikistan, and Uzbekistan. Evolving from the "Shanghai Five," which first met in 1996, SCO members agreed to jointly fight against what China referred to as the "three evils" of separatism, fundamentalism, and terrorism.[35] However, Russia and the PRC increasingly used the SCO to counter U.S. influence in Central Asia. China and Russia expanded SCO membership adding Iran, Pakistan, and India as observer nations. In 2005, the SCO issued a declaration calling for the United States to withdraw military forces from Central Asia, and in 2009 Kyrgyzstan nearly closed the U.S military base at Manas. China and Russia, working together, yield significant influence to impact regional and international politics relative to U.S. interests.

China and Russia also gradually improved economic ties. Russia-China bi-lateral trade increased from US $5.7 billion in 1999 to US $48 billion in 2010.[36] In 2011, China displaced Germany as Russia's largest trading partner. That same year, the two nations established a goal of increasing bilateral trade fourfold to $200 billion by 2020.[37] Russia increasingly exports energy resources to China as a major part of bi-lateral trade. From 1995 to 2007, Russia increased crude oil exports to China from 1,000 barrels per day (b/d) to 292,000 b/d.[38] Today, China is the world's second largest oil importer. Over 80% of Chinese crude oil imports originate from the Middle East while Russian crude oil makes up only 6% of China's imports.[39] In the future, China will increase oil imports from Russia to diversify away from potentially unstable sources in the Middle East. In 2011, Russia completed the first stage of the Eastern Siberia Pacific Ocean (ESPO) oil pipeline. The ESPO pipeline could potentially increase crude oil flow from Siberia to Northeast China by over a million b/d.[40]

Finally, China and Russia improved military relations, one of the most significant aspects of the strategic partnership. Moscow transferred arms to China as an enduring part of this military cooperation. According to analysis by the Stockholm International Peace Research Institute (SIPRI), China initiated large orders for naval equipment, combat aircraft, and air defense systems in 1992 responding to a Taiwanese procurement drive.[41] China turned to Russia because it lacked other potential suppliers following U.S. and European Union (EU) arms embargoes imposed in 1989.[42] From 1992 to 2007, Russia provided four-fifths of China's arms imports.[43] SIPRI analysts predict that China will be at least partially dependent on imports of Russian advanced weapons systems and technologies for the coming decade, especially aircraft and high performance, ship-launched, land attack missiles.[44]

More recently, China and Russia started conducting joint military exercises. The two countries have completed four Peace Mission exercises, in 2005, 2007, 2009, and 2010.[45] Begun as a bi-lateral military exercise between Russia and China, the two nations opened Peace Mission 2009 and 2010 to members of the SCO. The exercises began modestly, but China has increasingly gained valuable operational practice from the more experienced Russians.

During Peace Mission 2010, China exercised logistics capabilities moving large numbers of troops and equipment over long distances. China's J-10 multirole combat aircraft and H-6H bomber aircraft flew from western China to Kazakhstan and back, the longest non-stop, mid-air, refueled flight for any Chinese aircraft.[46] Western military analysts point out that the past two Peace Mission exercises exceeded counter-terrorism operations and are, in fact, ". . . pointed demonstrations of a capacity to intervene militarily against U.S. interests in Central Asia, the Korean Peninsula, or beyond."[47] Russia and China, through future joint exercises, will continue to build Chinese capacity and develop Sino-Russian joint interoperability. U.S. defense officials should be concerned about these trends, especially given the combined weight of Russian and Chinese conventional, nuclear, and cyber capabilities.

Similar to Sino-Russian relations during the Cold War, China and Russia also face challenges in their relationship. Despite resolving their territorial disputes, Russia has not returned land gained from China at the time of the unequal treaties. If China applies the same historical logic to Manchuria that it applied to the South China Sea, China could clash with Russia over Vladivostok, formerly China's eastern Maritime Province. The Russians are well aware of this possibility. Moscow constantly worries about Chinese illegal immigration to the Russian Far East, also referred to as the "Hanification" of Russia.[48] Overall, China and Russia maintain a level of fear and mistrust in their dealings with each other, a continuity of the history of Sino-Russian relations.

Moscow will also be tested as it develops further economic ties with China. Russia has prioritized development in the Russian Far East, but the government has made slow gains improving key infrastructure. Additionally, Russia's energy strategy in Asia suffers from some key shortfalls. Moscow plans to increase oil flow to Asia, but superior infrastructure and higher prices in European markets will make any shift to Asia difficult. Also, Russia, the world's leader in natural gas reserves, aims to export natural gas to China.[49] However, China has few plans to increase consumption of natural gas.

Russia and China will also be challenged to maintain the upward trend in military cooperation. Russia will increasingly see China's military expansion as a possible threat. As a result, Russia will be less willing to transfer certain military hardware and technology to China. At the same time, China will develop its own military industry freeing it from dependence on Russian military equipment.

Finally, as has been the case throughout history, broader geopolitics could alter the character of Sino-Russian relations. Currently, China and Russia share interests in Central Asia. However, Beijing and Moscow are also competing for influence in Central Asia. Russia attempts to hold a stronger position in this region through the Collective Security Treaty Organization (CSTO), of which China is not a member. For its part, China seeks to prevent Uighur separatism in Xinjiang originating from Central Asia. Beijing also looks to the region, specifically Kazakhstan, to mitigate future over dependence on Russian oil.[50] China is weary of Russia using energy like a weapon as it did against the Ukraine in 2006.

The United States, as well, could alter the course of Sino-Russian relations. According to Australian diplomat Bobo Lo, the greatest challenge to the existing Sino-Russian strategic partnership is that both China and Russia place a higher value on positive relations with the US than with each other.[51] U.S. bi-lateral relations with China and Russia are likely to shape Sino-Russian relations. If, for example, the US continues to isolate both China and Russia, the two countries will continue to strengthen their partnership. On the other hand, Moscow and Beijing will have to respond if the other significantly improves relations with the US. More indirectly, America also wields influence to change Russia's relationship with China through other Asian powers such as India and Japan.

The "strategic partnership" is the subject of much conjecture and debate. Richard Weitz has described it as *Strategic Parallelism Without Partnership or Passion* pointing out the limits of China-Russia cooperation.[52] On the other hand, Colin Gray emphasizes the strength of the relationship predicting a war between the United States and a China-Russia bloc.[53] As the United States considers the current situation, in the context of historical Sino-Russian relations, U.S. policymakers can only conclude that the strategic alliance between Russia and China is not a foregone conclusion, nor can it be discounted.

The United States cannot ignore the emerging Sino-Russian strategic partnership because America now faces a potential Cold War scenario in Asia. Whether China and Russia develop Sino-Russian relations as a limited partnership or a strong alliance, the United States must include Russia and Sino-Russian relations in any policy formulation for the Asia-Pacific. Outside powers will shape Sino-Russian relations in the future, just as they have in the past, and the United States remains the actor most capable of affecting the balance of China-Russia relations. When considering how America might approach China and Russia in the future, U.S. policymakers should start by looking into the past.

U.S. Cold War Strategy: Managing Sino-Russian Relations

The United States is compelled to influence relations between Beijing and Moscow, but this is not a new phenomenon for U.S. foreign policy. After Mao Zedong established the PRC in 1949, the US confronted a Sino-Soviet alliance in Asia for two decades. Similar to today, U.S. policy makers during the Cold War initially underestimated America's role in shaping Sino-Russian relations. George F. Kennan communicated the idea of Soviet containment in 1947 and U.S. strategy mistakenly placed China under an overarching umbrella of Soviet communism for the first two decades of the Cold War.[54] The US eventually learned to manage relations between China and Russia as a central part of a successful strategy for Asia. In the late 1960s, President Richard M. Nixon, along with Mao Zedong, carefully orchestrated a new era of US-China relations that radically shifted the Cold War balance of power in Asia. U.S. policy towards China and Russia during the Cold War evolved revealing insights for future U.S. strategy in Asia.

China and Russia formed the Sino-Soviet Alliance based on shared interests and common ideological ties.[55] After the Chinese Civil War ended, the PRC needed significant economic assistance. Mao Zedong held little optimism for U.S. support after America backed the

14

Nationalists during the Chinese Civil War. Ideologically, Beijing wanted to adopt a socialist economic model. Thus, Mao leaned toward the Soviet Union. In January 1950, Stalin signaled Soviet solidarity with China when Russian diplomats boycotted the United Nations (UN) after the UN failed to recognize the PRC. Shortly thereafter, Mao and Stalin signed the Sino-Soviet Treaty of Friendship in February 1950, which established a mutual defense alliance between the two nations.

Despite their alliance, China and Russia maintained uneasy relations reflecting historical tensions. Mao traveled to Russia, his first official state visit outside of China, to negotiate the Sino-Soviet treaty in December 1949. Stalin hardly embraced China's communist leader ignoring Mao for days at a time.[56] After months of negotiations, the two leaders signed the agreement, but Stalin forced Mao to surrender territorial concessions in Manchuria and Xinjiang. The Soviet Union also extended Russian use of Dalian Harbor and the Lushun Naval Base.[57] After Stalin's death, Mao accused Stalin of attempting to establish "semi-colonies" on Chinese territory.[58]

The US projected China's lean towards the Soviet Union, but U.S. policymakers questioned the strength of Sino-Russian relations. In late 1948, President Harry S. Truman and his staff conducted a policy review for China. They predicted that China would not necessarily align with the Soviet Union given Mao's relative independence from the Soviets throughout the Chinese Civil War. Truman's staff anticipated that China would likely follow the path of Yugoslavian leader Josip Broz Tito. Tito broke with the Soviet Union accepting U.S. economic assistance earlier in June.[59]

Truman's advisors detected friction between China and the Soviet Union, but did little to shape their relations. Overall, the group concluded that the loss of China to communism would not be a net gain for the Soviet Union. Future Secretary of State Dean Acheson summarized

U.S. policy towards the PRC when he recommended that the administration "wait till the dust settles."[60] Ironically, over a year after the dust settled, it was Acheson who laid out what Henry Kissinger describes as a "sweeping new Asia policy."[61]

In a January 1950 speech to the National Press Club, Secretary of State Acheson proposed alignment of U.S. and Chinese interests based on the common threat from the Soviet Union.[62] He argued that the imperialist aims of the Soviet Union provided a greater threat to China than the United States. However, Acheson made his proposal too late. The United States could not pursue Acheson's policy recommendation because China entered the Korean War. After Chinese military forces entered the war, the US increasingly treated the PRC and Soviet Union as a single communist monolith. However, Moscow and Beijing grew further apart.

U.S. strategists for Asia missed some early opportunities to shape Sino-Russian relations in favor of the United States, but American foreign policymakers eventually seized upon opportunities presented by the gradual evolution of the Sino-Soviet split. China and Russia began to split almost from the beginning of their alliance. Fostering suspicion and mistrust, Joseph Stalin manipulated China during the Korean War. When North Korean leader Kim Il Sung requested Soviet support for the initial invasion of South Korea, Stalin directed Kim to get permission from Mao Zedong in an attempt to shift responsibility for the war to China.[63] At the same time, Stalin initially kept Soviet forces out of the war convincing both Mao and Kim that Russian forces needed to prepare for a greater threat in Europe. Stalin eventually supplied massive military aid to China and North Korea to include Soviet military advisors, artillery equipment, and air units.[64] However, according to John Lewis Gaddis, Stalin supported Mao and Kim because he wanted to prolong the war to keep the U.S. military tied down in East Asia. Gaddis points out that China and North Korea sought to end the war as early as the fall of 1952, but could not gain Soviet approval until after Stalin's death in 1953. [65]

After Stalin, Nikita Khrushchev undermined the ideological basis of the Sino-Soviet alliance. In February 1956, Khrushchev delivered a secret speech to the 20th Congress of the Communist Party denouncing Stalin and promoting "peaceful co-existence" between communism and capitalism.[66] Khrushchev promoted de-Stalinization revising the historical basis of communist revolution, and at the same time he undermined Beijing's domestic control. Mao watched as Warsaw Pact members challenged Soviet authority in reaction to de-Stalinization. In June 1956, large scale riots broke out in Poland against the Polish Communist Party who had released political prisoners and removed Stalinists from power in response to Khrushchev's policy revision. Later in July, a popular movement in Hungary rebelled against the Soviet backed Hungarian leadership. The Soviet military, under pressure from Mao Zedong, responded killing approximately 20,000 Hungarians.[67] The PRC and the Soviet Union formed their alliance in the context of shared socialist identities, but now the two countries grew ideologically apart.

Soviet revisionism increasingly threatened China, so Mao Zedong pursued domestic and foreign policy that was more and more out of step with the Soviet Union. In May of 1958, Mao unveiled the Great Leap Forward to the 8th CCP Congress. With the Great Leap, the CCP attempted to pursue economic development through revolutionary social change, a stark contrast to the more cautious Soviet approach. In August, the People's Liberation Army began the Second Taiwan Strait Crisis shelling the Taiwanese offshore islands of Quemoy and Matsu.[68] Later in 1959, China and India clashed along their disputed border and Khrushchev refused to support Chinese claims calling the conflict "stupid."[69] Mao had intensified the Sino-Soviet split by undermining Nikita Khrushchev's policy of peaceful co-existence, and he threatened to drag the Soviet Union unwillingly into a major conflict as a result of his radical foreign policy.

17

By the early 1960s, Beijing and Moscow overtly displayed evidence of the Sino-Soviet split. In September, Moscow recalled Soviet advisors back from China. Russian nuclear scientists helping China develop an atomic bomb tore up their documents and returned home.[70] Later in October 1961, Chinese Premier Zhou Enlai walked out of the Soviet party congress after Khrushchev criticized Chinese communism.[71] The United States recognized the Sino-Soviet division, but U.S. policy did not shift for another decade. Throughout the years of major U.S. military involvement in Vietnam, therefore, U.S. policymakers failed to capitalize on the decay in Sino-Soviet relations while both China and Russia supported North Vietnam.

Eventually, the United States and China improved relations as both nations reconsidered national interests. According to Lorenz Luthi, Mao Zedong reevaluated his own radical domestic and foreign policies because they had prevented China from attaining great power status. Domestically, Mao realized that the Great Leap Forward and Cultural Revolution had to give way to more pragmatic economic policies that would allow China to integrate into the world economy. At the same time, China sought to repair its international reputation by improving diplomatic relations and withdrawing support to global revolutions.[72]

Mao also reconsidered the China-Russia security alliance as Sino-Russian relations evolved. Despite losing Soviet technical support, China developed and tested its first nuclear bomb in October 1964, alleviating China's dependence on Soviet nuclear capabilities. Later in 1969, the Soviet Union massed 42 divisions along the China-Russia border after the two nations clashed at the disputed border along the Ussuri River. Moscow considered nuclear options, and Soviet diplomats contacted U.S. officials to measure America's response to a possible Soviet strike against Chinese nuclear weapons facilities.[73] In the context of China's global ambitions and the Sino-Soviet border conflict, Mao Zedong began to see improved relations with the United States as a strategic necessity.[74]

In the United States, newly elected President Richard M. Nixon considered US-China relations in the midst of a failing war in Vietnam. He defined U.S. priorities as ending the war in Vietnam and re-establishing U.S. dominance in the Cold War.[75] To achieve this, Nixon aimed to re-align the geo-political landscape in Asia. The president published an article in Foreign Affairs in October 1967 advocating reconciliation between China and the United States, an overture well known to Mao Zedong.[76] Richard Nixon seized his opportunity to shift U.S. policy during the Sino-Soviet border clash. Nixon directed his staff to maintain a neutral position on the border conflict, but "lean towards China."[77]

In the years that followed, Nixon managed a complex and delicate courtship between the US and China. After rounds of secret communications and ping pong diplomacy, President Nixon made his official visit to Beijing in February 1972. During the visit, China and the US agreed to the Shanghai Communique normalizing bi-lateral relations and establishing the U.S. One-China Policy.

President Nixon made a significant impact on the Sino-Soviet relationship altering the course of the Cold War. After the Vietnam War, the United States and China cooperated to counter "Soviet hegemony" in Asia and Central Asia. In 1978, the US and PRC exercised parallel efforts to counter the Soviet-backed Vietnamese invasion of Cambodia. In Afghanistan, the US and China supported Mujahedeen groups against invading Soviet forces.[78] John Lewis Gaddis highlights the impact of Nixon's accomplishment claiming that, "He [Nixon] could exert 'leverage' – always a good thing to have in international relations – by 'tilting' as needed toward the Soviet Union or China, who were by then so hostile to one another that they competed for Washington's favor."[79] President Nixon, recognizing the importance of Sino-Russian relations on geopolitics in Asia, altered the character of U.S. relations with China, effectively counter balancing the Soviet Union. By doing so, Nixon took a major step towards re-establishing America's position in the Cold War.

During the Cold War, America successfully managed the triangular relationship between the US, China, and the Soviet Union. Early on, China and Russia set aside their differences forming an alliance against a common enemy, the United States. The US responded altering Sino-Russian relations and shifting the geo-political landscape in Asia. In contrast to current U.S. policymakers, Richard Nixon not only appreciated the importance of China-Russia relations, but he also successfully managed Sino-Russian relations in pursuit of U.S. strategy.

The current context of US-China-Russia relations is different than it was in 1972, but the U.S. requirement to manage China and Russia in Asia remains the same. The Soviet Union enjoyed a position of strength over the US and China in the early 1970s. Therefore, the US and China formed an alliance against the Soviet Union as a result of US-China shared security interests. Today, the United States is in a position of relative strength and China and Russia are forming a strategic partnership to counter the US. America is in the midst of a strategic shift towards Asia. Like President Nixon during the Cold War, U.S. policymakers must formulate a grand strategy to manage China and Russia as part of this shift.

The U.S. Pivot towards Asia: Managing Russia and China

What does a "pivot" towards Asia mean? Kenneth G. Lieberthal, director of the John L. Thornton China Center at The Brookings Institute, recently outlined four dimensions of the U.S. pivot towards Asia compiled from Obama Administration policy statements. First, the US will deepen economic liberalization in the region through the development of the Trans Pacific Partnership. Second, despite serious budget cuts, America will maintain its military presence in Asia. As part of this, the US will begin rotational deployment of Marines to Darwin, Australia and reduce U.S. forces permanently stationed in Europe. Third, America will make diplomatic

20

efforts to develop multi-lateral security frameworks such as the East Asia Summit, a relatively new regional organization forming for East Asia. Finally, the US will commit to promoting human rights and democracy.[80] Although the Administration does not advertise as such, the US is pivoting towards Asia to manage China.

The preceding analysis commends some broad recommendations for future U.S. China policy. First, the United States should consider Sino-Russian relations when formulating policy for China. U.S. policy since the end of the Cold War underestimated the significance of China-Russia relations. During this time, China and Russia developed their current "strategic partnership." The Sino-Russian partnership could be good or bad for future U.S. interests in Asia. Unlike the past twenty years, however, the US must shape future relations between Russia and China as part of a comprehensive approach to the region.

The second recommendation is related to the first. U.S. policymakers must recognize Russia as an Asian power. Russia is a traditional Asian power, and Moscow is increasing its influence in the Asia-Pacific. As a start, American strategists should adjust current conceptions that Russia is only a European country. As a practical measure towards this end, the US could update the Unified Campaign Plan to place the Russian military's Joint Strategic Command (JSC) East into the PACOM area of operation.[81] At the same time, U.S. policymakers should not rush to diminish Russia's role in Europe. Former U.S. National Security Advisor Zbigniew Brzezinski recently argued that expanding the west, to include incorporating Russia into the EU, could provide America an effective method to balance against China in the East.[82]

Third, the United States should carefully manage the US-China-Russia triangular relationship. As Russia and China strive to create a multi-polar world, the United States should counter by returning to great power politics. Russia increasingly sees itself as a possible swing state in a bi-polar conflict between the US and China. Thus, U.S. foreign policymakers are faced

21

with important decisions. America could seek improved relations with Russia to balance against China. President Nixon successfully employed this balancing strategy during the Cold War. It is equally possible, however, that the US could align with both Russia and China against a common enemy such as Islamic extremism. Moreover, America should avoid unnecessarily pursuing policies that push Russia and China away from the US and closer to each other.

Finally, the United States needs to take a broad view of its foreign policy. Since the end of the Cold War, U.S. policy failed to coordinate strategy for Europe and Asia. Instead of dividing China and Russia into separate strategies, the United States should develop grand strategy synchronizing the two.

Conclusion

As the United States pivots toward the Asia-Pacific, it is essential that U.S. policymakers include Sino-Russian relations in any strategy formulation for China. The United States successfully managed US-China-Russia relations during the Cold War. However, since the end of the Cold War, the US has ignored Russia's role as an Asian power leaving Moscow out of U.S. strategy for the Asia-Pacific. Instead, the US pursued two separate and disconnected strategies; one isolated Russia in Europe while the other contained China in Asia. All the while, China and Russia drifted away from America and toward each other as they developed a new strategic partnership. Today, Beijing and Moscow yield significant global influence through the current strategic partnership. In the future, China and Russia could transform their partnership into an alliance, threatening U.S. interests in the region. The US intends to counter the rise of China by making a strategic pivot towards the Asia-Pacific. Going forward, American policymakers and strategists must recognize that Sino-Russian relations, past and present, are an essential aspect of dealing with China.

Notes

[1] Barak Obama, *Sustaining U.S. Global Leadership: Priorities for the 21st Century Defense*, 2012, 2.

[2] Both Colin Gray and Michael Levin have written about the possibility of a future U.S. war against China and Russia. See Colin S. Gray, *Another Bloody Century* (London: Phoenix, 2005) and Michael L. Levin, *The Next Great Clash China and Russia Vs. the United States*. (Westport, Connecticut: Prager Security International, 2008).

[3] Richard Weitz, "Russia, China End Decades-Long Border Dispute," *World Politics Review Online*, August 1, 2008, http://www.worldpoliticsreview.com/articles/2517/russia-china-end-decades-long-border-dispute (accessed March 15, 2012)

[4] Michael G. Nosov, "Russia between Europe and Asia: Some Aspects of Russia's Asian Policy," *Russia between East and West: Russian Foreign Policy on the Threshold of the Twenty-First Century,* ed.Gabriel Gorodetsky (London: Frank Cass, 2003), 171.

[5] David Mack, "Eastern Promises: Russia's Plan to Develop Siberia" *CSIS Report* http://csis.org/blog/eastern-promises-russia%E2%80%99s-plan-develop-siberia (Accessed March 15, 2011)

[6] Dmitri Trenin, "Russia Reborn." *Foreign Affairs* 88, no. 6 (Nov/Dec 2009): 64-78.

[7] R.K.I. Quested, *The Expansion of Russia in East Asia 1857-1860*, (Kuala Lumpur: University of Malaya Press, 1968), 285.

[8] Russia signed three treaties with China: the Treaty of Aigun (May 1858), the Treaty of Tientsin (June 1858), and Treaty of Peking (November 1860).

[9] R.K.I Quested, *Sino-Russian Relations: A Short History* (Sydney: George Allen and Unwin Publishers, 1984), 111.

[10] Tienfong Cheng, *A History of Sino-Russian Relations* (Washington D.C.: Public Affairs Press, 1957), 280. For more background on Soviet influence in Mongolia, which began in the 1920s, see Cheng's chapter entitled "The Soviet Union and Outer Mongolia" p. 160-167.

[11] See Gilbert Rozman, "Russian Repositioning in Northeast Asia: Putin's Impact and Current Prospects" *Russia's Prospects in Asia*, ed.Stephen Blank (Carlisle, PA: Strategic Studies Institute, 2010), 63-96. See also Dmitri Trenin, "Russia Leaves the West," *Foreign Affairs* 85, no. 4 (Jul/Aug 2006): 87-96. See also Jeffrey, Mankoff. *Russian Foreign Policy*, 2nd ed. (Lanham, MD: Rowman & Littlefield Publishers, Inc., 2012).

[12] William Clinton, *A National Security Strategy of Engagement and Enlargement*, 1995.

[13] Robert Willard, "Statement of Admiral Robert F. Willard, U.S. Navy Commander, U.S. Pacific Command before the House Armed Services Committee on U.S. Pacific Command Posture," April 6, 2011. http://armed-services.senate.gov/statemnt/2011/04%20April/Willard%2004-12-11.pdf (Accessed February 23, 2012)

[14] Rozman, 88.

[15] Barak Obama, *National Security Strategy*, 2010.

[16] Henry Kissinger, *On China* (New York: The Penguin Press, 2011), 528.

[17] William S. Cohen, *The United States Security Strategy for the Asia-Pacific Region*, 1998

[18] Sustaining Global Leadership, 3.

[19] Hillary Clinton, "America's Pacific Century," *Foreign Policy Magazine Online*, November 2011, http://www.foreignpolicy.com/articles/2011/10/11/americas_pacific_century (accessed March 15, 2012).

[20] William Clinton, 27.

[21] Charles Kupchan, "NATO's Final Frontier," *Foreign Affairs* 89 no. 3 (May/Jun 2010) 100-112.

[22] Trenin, Russia Reborn, 64-78.

[23] James M. Goldgeier, "Prospects for U.S. Russia Cooperation," *Russia After the Fall,* ed.Andrew Kutchins (Washington D.C.: Carnegie Endowment for International Peace, 2002), 278.

[24] Russia, for example, is a member of the Six Party Talks but carries little influence.

[25] Unified Campaign Plan http://www.defense.gov/home/features/2009/0109_unifiedcommand/ (Accessed March 29, 2012).

[26] PACOM SFG's were 1) China, 2) India, 3) North Korea, 4) Allies and Partners, and 5) Transnational Threats

[27] Bobo Lo, *Axis of Convenience* (London: Royal Institute of International Affairs, 2008), 174.

[28] Kupchan, 100-112.

[29] R. Craig Nation, "Russia in East Asia: Aspirations and Limitations," *Russia's Prospects in Asia*, ed.Stephen Blank (Carlisle, PA: Strategic Studies Institute, 2010), 38.

[30] Weitz, 1.

[31] Nation, 38.

[32] Russia and China released the first anti-hegemony statement in 1991. See Jennifer Anderson, *The Limits of Sino-Russian Partnership*, (London: The International Institute for strategic Studies, 1997), 15-20.

[33] Ministry of Foreign Affairs People's Republic of China, *Joint Statement of The People's Republic of China and the Russian Federation on Major International Issues*, 23 May 2008. http://www.fmprc.gov.cn/eng/wjdt/2649/t465821.htm (accessed March 7, 2012).

[34] Minxin Pei, "Why Beijing Votes with Moscow," *NYTimes.com*, February 7, 2012,

http://www.nytimes.com/2012/02/08/opinion/why-beijing-votes-with-moscow.html

(Accessed April 9, 2012).

[35] Chien-peng Chung, "The Shanghai Co-Operation Organization: China's Changing Influence in

Central Asia." *The China Quarterly*, no. 180 (Dec): 989-1009.

[36] Lo, 35.

[37] James Brooke, "China, Russia Vow to Quadruple Trade this Decade," *Voice of America*

Online, June 17, 2011. http://www.voanews.com/english/news/economy-and-

business/China-Russia-Vow-to-Quadruple-Trade-This-Decade-124101304.html. (Accessed

March 25, 2012).

[38] Erica S. Downs, "Sino-Russian Energy Relations: An uncertain courtship," *The Future of*

China -Russia Relations: Asia in the new Millennium, ed.James Bellequa (Lexington, KY:

University Press of Kentucky), 148.

[39] Zhang Jian, "China's Energy Security: Prospects, Challenges, and Opportunities," *The*

Brookings Institute, Center for Northeast Asian Policy Studies, July 2011, 17.

[40] Ibid, 153.

[41] Linda Jakobson, Paul Holtom, Dean Knox, and Jianchao Peng, "China's Energy and Security

Relations with Russia: Hopes, Frustrations, and Uncertainties," *SIPRI Policy Paper*, no.29

(Oct 2011), 16.

[42] Ibid

[43] Richard Lotspeich, "Economic Integration of China and Russia in the Post-Soviet Era," *The*

Future of China -Russia Relations: Asia in the new Millennium, ed.James Bellequa

(Lexington, KY: University Press of Kentucky), 112.

[44] SIPRI, 17.

[45] SIPRI, 25.

[46] Ibid.

[47] SIPRI, 25.

[48] Lo, 179-180.

[49] Ibid, 136.

[50] SIPRI, 28.

[51] Lo, 36.

[52] See Richard Weitz, *China Russia Security Relations: Strategic Parallelism without Partnership Or Passion?* (Carlisle, PA: Strategic Studies Institute, 2008).

[53] See Colin S. Gray, *Another Bloody Century* (London: Phoenix, 2005).

[54] George, Kennan, "The Sources of Soviet Conduct" *Foreign Affairs* 25, no. 4 (Jul 1947): 566.

[55] For discussion on the role of ideology in Sino-Soviet relations see Chen Jian, *Mao's China & the Cold War* (Chapel Hill, NC: The University of North Carolina Press, 2001). Also see Lorenz Luthi, *The Sino-Soviet Split: Cold War in the Communist World* (Princeton, NJ: Princeton University Press, 2008).

[56] Kissinger, 115.

[57] The agreement established Soviet use of Lushun Naval Base until 1952.

[58] Kissinger, 117.

[59] John Lewis Gaddis, *The Cold War: A New History* (New York: The Penguin Press, 2005), 33.

[60] Ibid, 37.

[61] Kissinger, 118.

[62] Acheson later was criticized for contributing to the Korean War by leaving Korea out of U.S. interests in Asia during this same speech.

[63] Zhihua Shen and Danhui Li, *After Leaning to One Side: China and its Allies in the Cold War*, (Washington D.C.: Woodrow Wilson Center Press, 2011), 31.

[64] Ibid, 96.

[65] Gaddis, 60.

[66] Tsuyoshi Hasegawa, "Introduction: East Asia-the Second Significant Front of the Cold War," *The Cold War in East Asia 1945-1991*, ed.Tsuyoshi Hasegawa (Stanford, CA: Woodrow Wilson Center Press, 2011), 6.

[67] Gaddis, 108-109.

[68] Kissinger 172-180.

[69] Jonathan Spence. *The Search for Modern China*. (New York: W.W. Norton & Company, 1999), 557.

[70] Soviet scientist went to China as part of an agreement between Mao and Khrushchev in 1957. The Chinese developed the bomb in October 1964. See Spence, 567.

[71] Spence, 559.

[72] Lorenz Luthi, "Chinese Foreign Policy, 1960-1979," *The Cold War in East Asia 1945-1991* ed.Tsuyoshi Hasegawa (Stanford, CA: Woodrow Wilson Center Press, 2011), 152-171.

[73] Kissinger, 218-220.

[74] Ibid, 213.

[75] Ibid.

[76] Richard Nixon, "Asia After Vietnam" *Foreign Affairs* 46, no. 1 (Oct 1967): 111.

[77] Kissinger, 215-221.

[78] John Garver, *Foreign Relations of the People's Republic of China* (Upper Saddle River, NJ: Prentice Hall, 1993), 70-94.

[79] Gaddis, 155.

[80] Kenneth Lieberthal, Richard Bush, Jonathan Pollack, "Understanding the U.S. Pivot to Asia," by Thomas J. Christensen, *The Brookings Institution*, January 31, 2012, 4-11, http://www.brookings.edu/~/media/Files/events/2012/0131_us_asia/20120131_us_asia_panel_one.pdfhttp://www.brookings.edu/~/media/Files/events/2012/0131_us_asia/20120131_pivot_asia.pdf. (Accessed March 20, 2012)

[81] In October 2010 the Russian military reorganized into four new Joint Strategic Commands (East, West, South, and Centre). See Janes Security Assessment – Russia and the CIS.

[82] Zbigniew Brzezinski, "Balancing the East, Upgrading the West: U.S. Grand Strategy in an Age of Upheaval." *Foreign Affairs* 91, no.1 (Jan/Feb 2012): 97-104.

Bibliography

The White House, *National Security Strategy*, May 2010.

Anderson, Jennifer. *The Limits of Sino-Russian Strategic Partnership*. London: The International Institute for Strategic Studies, 1997.

Bellacqua, James, ed. *The Future of China-Russia Relations: Asia in the New Millennium*. Lexington, KY: University Press of Kentucky, 2010.

Blank, Stephen J., ed. *Russia's Prospects in Asia*. Carlisle, PA: Strategic Studies Institute, 2010.

Chen, Jian. *Mao's China & the Cold War*. Chapel Hill, NC: The University of North Carolina Press, 2001.

Cheng, Tienfong. *A History of Sino-Russian Relations*. Washington D.C.: Public Affairs Press, 1957.

Chung, Chien-Peng. "The Shanghai Co-Operation Organization: China's Changing Influence in Central Asia." *The China Quarterly*, no. 180 (Dec): 989-1009.

Gaddis, John Lewis. *The Cold War: A New History*. New York: The Penguin Press, 2005.

Garver, John W. *Foreign Relations of the People's Republic of China*. Upper Saddle River, NJ: Prentice Hall, 1993.

Gorodetsky, Gabriel, ed. *Russia between East and West: Russian Foreign Policy on the Threshold of the Twenty-First Century*. London: Frank Cass, 2003.

Gray, Colin S. *Another Bloody Century*. London: Phoenix, 2005.

Hasegawa, Tsuyoshi, ed. *The Cold War in East Asia 1945-1991*. Stanford, CA: Woodrow Wilson Center Press, 2011.

Kennan, George "The Sources of Soviet Conduct" Foreign Affairs 25, no. 4 (Jul 1947).

Kissinger, Henry. *On China*. New York: The Penguin Press, 2011.

Kupchan, Charles. "NATO's Final Frontier." *Foreign Affairs* 89, no. 3 (May/Jun): 100-112.

Kutchins, Andrew C., ed. *Russia After the Fall*. Washington D.C.: Carnegie Endowment for International Peace, 2002.

Levin, Michael L. *The Next Great Clash China and Russia Vs. the United States*. Westport, Connecticut: Prager Security International, 2008.

Lieberthal, Kenneth, Richard Bush, Jonathan Pollack, "Understanding the U.S. Pivot to Asia," by Thomas J. Christensen, *The Brookings Institution*, January 31, 2012, 4-11, http://www.brookings.edu/~/media/Files/events/2012/0131_us_asia/20120131_us_asia_panel _one.pdfhttp://www.brookings.edu/~/media/Files/events/2012/0131_us_asia/20120131_pivot _asia.pdf. (Accessed March 20, 2012).

Lo, Bobo. *Axis of Convenience: Moscow, Beijing, and the New Geopolitics*. London: Royal Institute of International Affairs, 2008.

Luthi, Lorenz M. *The Sino-Soviet Split: Cold War in the Communist World*. Princeton, NJ: Princeton University Press, 2008.

Mack, David. "Eastern Promises: Russia's Plan to Develop Siberia" *CSIS Report*, http://csis.org/blog/eastern-promises-russia%E2%80%99s-plan-develop-siberi. (Accessed March 15, 2012).

Mankoff, Jeffrey. *Russian Foreign Policy*. Second Edition ed. Lanham, MD: Rowman & Littlefield Publishers, Inc., 2012.

Nixon, Richard. "Asia After Vietnam" *Foreign Affairs* 46, no. 1 (Oct 1967): 111.

Obama, Barak, *Sustaining U.S. Global Leadership: Priorities for the 21st Century Defense*, 2012.

Pei, Minxin. "Why Beijing Votes with Moscow," *NYTimes.com*, February 7, 2012.

http://www.nytimes.com/2012/02/08/opinion/why-beijing-votes-with-moscow.html

(Accessed April 9, 2012).

Quested, R. K. I. *The Expansion of Russia in East Asia 1857-1860*. Kuala Lumpur: University of

Malaya Press, 1968.

Quested, R. K. I. *Sino-Russian Relations: A Short History*. Sydney: George Allen and Unwin

Publishers, 1984.

Shaofeng, Chen. "Has China's Foreign Energy Quest Enhanced its Energy Security?" *The China

Quarterly* 207: 600.

Shen, Zhihua, and Danhui Li. *After Leaning to One Side: China and its Allies in the Cold War*.

Washington D.C.: Woodrow Wilson Center Press, 2011.

Spence, Jonathan D. *The Search for Modern China*. 2nd Edition ed. New York: W.W. Norton &

Company, 1999.

Trenin, Dmitri. "Russia Reborn." *Foreign Affairs* 88, no. 6 (Nov/Dec 2009): 64-78.

Trenin, Dmitri. "Russia Leaves the West." *Foreign Affairs* 85, no. 4 (Jul/Aug 2006): 87-96.

Weitz, Richard. *China Russia Security Relations: Strategic Parallelism without Partnership or

Passion?* Carlisle, PA: Strategic Studies Institute, 2008.

Weitz, Richard. "Russia, China End Decades-Long Border Dispute." *World Politics Review

Online*, August 1, 2008, http://www.worldpoliticsreview.com/articles/2517/russia-china-

end-decades-long-border-dispute (accessed March 15, 2012).

Willard, Robert, "Statement of Admiral Robert F. Willard, U.S. Navy Commander, U.S. Pacific

Command before the House Armed Services Committee on U.S. Pacific Command Posture,"

April 6, 2011. http://armed-services.senate.gov/statemnt/2011/04%20April/Willard%2004-

12-11.pdf (Accessed February 23, 2012).